The Changing Seasons
Winter

Paul Humphrey

W
FRANKLIN WATTS

First published in 2007 by
Franklin Watts

© 2007 Franklin Watts

Franklin Watts
338 Euston Road
London NW1 3BH

Franklin Watts Australia
Level 17/207 Kent Street
Sydney, NSW 2000

A CIP catalogue record for this book is available from the British Library

Dewey classification number: 578.4'3

ISBN: 978 0 7496 7165 5

Planning and production by Discovery Books Limited
Editors: Paul Humphrey, Rebecca Hunter
Designer: Jemima Lumley

Photo credits: Cardiff Council (Cardiff Winter Wonderland): title page, 11;
CFW Images/Chris Fairclough: 18, 19, 24, 27; Corbis: 16; Chris Fairclough:
front cover, 10, 12, 13, 28, 29; FLPA: 4, 9 (John Watkins), 15 (S & D & K
Maslowski), 17 (Terry Whittaker), 20 (Jan Vermeer/Foto Natura); Getty
Images: 8 (Scott Markewitz/Aurora); 24 (Photonica); Rebecca Hunter: 6, 7;
Istockphoto.com: 14 and back cover (Cheryl Triplett), 22 (Elena Elisseeva),
25 top (Kelly Cline), 26; Photodisc: 21; Photographers Direct: 23 (Oli Gardner).

Printed in China

Franklin Watts is a division of Hachette Children's Books,
an Hachette Livre UK company.

Contents

Winter is the season that follows autumn.

Many trees have lost
all their leaves.

It is often rainy in winter.

Sometimes there are floods.

 We can play
winter games ...

... or go ice skating.

 # It is dark and cold in the evenings.

We spend more
time indoors.

13

 # There are lots of berries on the bushes.

Berries make good
winter food for birds.

 Some animals grow a thick winter coat.

Others hibernate until
spring comes.

 By the middle of winter it can get very cold with frost or snow.

It is fun to build
a snowman.

You can see animal tracks in the snow.

 These are rabbit tracks.

 # Ponds freeze up ...

... and ducks skid
on the ice.

23

 We get cold when
we play outside in
the snow ...

... but we can
eat warm winter
food afterwards.

 Near the end of winter, we see new lambs in the fields.

Snowdrops appear.
Spring is coming!

Winter projects

Pantomime puppets

Many people go to see a pantomime in winter. This project shows you how to make your own pantomime theatre and puppets.

You will need:

Old wooden spoons ❋ Acrylic paints ❋ Pieces of fabric and wool
Some stiff cardboard ❋ A large cardboard box ❋ Glue ❋ Sticky tape
Two large pieces of coloured crêpe paper

What to do:

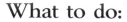

1. Paint faces on the backs of the wooden spoons.
2. Cut out some body shapes from the cardboard.
3. Cut out some clothes shapes from the fabric and glue them to the body shapes.

4. Glue or tape the body shapes and clothes to the handles of the spoons.

5. Cut a large hole in the side of the cardboard box. This will be your stage.

6. Cut away the other side of the cardboard box, so that you can see all the way through.

7. Cover the rest of the box in one of the sheets of crêpe paper.

8. Use the second piece of crêpe paper to make curtains for your stage. Now you can put on a show!

28

Make a bird feeder

Birds often find it hard to find food in winter.
You can help them by making this easy feeder.

You will need:
An empty plastic drinks bottle ❄ Some strong string
A few wooden sticks ❄ Scissors or a sharp knife
A large bag of unsalted peanuts

What to do:

1. Ask an adult to help you cut some slits in the bottle.

2. Push the sticks through the slits so the birds will have something to perch on.

3. Fill the bottle with nuts and put the top back on.

4. Tie the string around the bottle top and hang the bottle from the branch of a tree.

5. Don't forget to fill the feeder up each day. Once the birds start using your feeder, they will come back each day for more food.

6. Record which birds visit your feeder.

Index

BRITAIN in ROMAN TIMES

Tim Locke

W
FRANKLIN WATTS
LONDON • SYDNEY

© 2003 Franklin Watts

First published in 2003 by
Franklin Watts
96 Leonard Street
London
EC2A 4XD

Franklin Watts Australia
45-51 Huntley Street
NSW 2015
Australia

ISBN: 0 7496 4870 8

A CIP catalogue record for this book is available from the British Library

Printed in Malaysia
Planning and production by Discovery Books Limited
Editor: Helen Dwyer
Design: Keith Williams
Picture research: Rachel Tisdale

Photographs:
Cover, title page and border British Museum, 4 Discovery Books Picture Library/Alex
Ramsay, 5 bottom C M Dixon, 6 Discovery Books Picture Library/Alex Ramsay, 7
Ermine Street Guard, 8 English Heritage/Ivan Lapper, 9 top Discovery Books Picture
Library/Alex Ramsay, 9 bottom Discovery Books Picture Library/Alex Ramsay, 10 &
11 left C M Dixon, 11 right English Heritage/Jonathan Bailey, 12, 13 top, 13 bottom,
14, 15 top, 15 bottom & 16 C M Dixon, 17 left English Heritage/John Critchley, 17
right English Heritage/Jonathan Bailey, 18 & 19 top C M Dixon, 19 bottom
Discovery Books Picture Library, 20 Ermine Street Guard, 21 top C M Dixon, 21
bottom, 22 & 23 top C M Dixon, 23 bottom & 24 Discovery Books Picture
Library/Alex Ramsay, 25 top C M Dixon, 25 bottom Colchester Archaeological Trust,
26 C M Dixon, 27 left Discovery Books Picture Library/Alex Ramsay, 27 right English
Heritage/Jonathan Bailey, 28 & 29 top Discovery Books Picture Library/Alex Ramsay,
29 bottom Chris Butler

BRITAIN in ROMAN TIMES

Contents

Roman Britain

The city of Rome was founded in central Italy about 2,750 years ago. Within five hundred years the people of Rome – the Romans – had conquered all Italy. The Romans had the most powerful army and navy in the world. With it they captured lands across Europe and North Africa, building a huge empire. Then in AD 43 – nearly 2,000 years ago – the Romans invaded Britain.

Before the Romans arrived, the people of Britain belonged to many tribes, each ruled by their own kings and queens. When the Romans arrived, some tribes made peace while others fought the invaders. But soon the Romans had conquered much of Britain and the island slowly began to change.

Roman influences

A few of the Britons became rich as they traded with the Roman army and the new Roman towns. Some went on living in the same circular huts as their ancestors had done, but others built rectangular, Roman-style houses. The Britons began to use everyday Roman items like door locks and drinking glasses in their homes.

◄ The British tribes lived in round huts like these modern life-size replicas at Butser Ancient Farm in Hampshire. Inside each hut was one large room, with a fire in the middle, from which smoke rose through the thatched roof.

Towns that were also ports

Other major towns

Major forts

Major roads

ANTONINE WALL

Corbridge
Carlisle
Newcastle-upon-Tyne
HADRIAN'S WALL

Aldborough
York

Chester
Lincoln

Brancaster

Wroxeter
Leicester
Caistor-by-Norwich
Burgh Castle

Colchester
Walton Castle

Gloucester
St Albans
Bradwell

Caerwent
Cirencester
London
Reculver

Caerleon
Richborough

Bath
Silchester
Canterbury
Dover

Winchester
Lympne

Portchester
Pevensey

Exeter
Dorchester
Chichester

Everyone who owned property – houses, farms, land, animals and **slaves** – had to pay money as taxes to Rome. These taxes made the Roman **empire** very rich.

▼This tombstone from Colchester (now in Colchester Castle Museum) shows an invading Roman soldier's horse treading on a Briton.

🛡 LANGUAGE

The Britons spoke a Celtic language similar to the Welsh spoken today, but they did not write anything down. A language called Latin was used all over the Roman Empire, although most people spoke their local language too. Some Britons learned to read and write Latin.

The Roman Army

The Roman empire had a very strong army, made up of soldiers from all over the empire. In Britain the Roman army's first job was to control the British tribes, but its soldiers also built forts, bridges, roads and some of the first towns.

The northern edge of the empire in Britain was near the present border between England and Scotland. There, between AD 122 and 127 the army built a huge wall that we today call Hadrian's Wall, to keep out invaders from the north and to mark the northern boundary of their empire. All along the wall were forts and small castles.

Life in the Roman army

The army was divided into groups, or legions, of about 6,000 men called legionaries. To join a legion you had to be a Roman citizen (a free man with the right to vote in Rome) or the son of a legionary. Others could become soldiers called auxiliaries. They were paid less than legionaries, though they often had special skills like horse-riding, swimming or fighting with bows and arrows.

▼ Much of Hadrian's Wall can still be seen today. In the forts along it were bath houses, store rooms and dormitories (sleeping quarters) for 9,500 soldiers.

▼Modern replicas of the armour and weapons of a Roman legionary in Britain, worn here by a member of the Ermine Street Guard, a Roman re-enactment society. A legionary had to pay for his uniform out of his wages.

BUILDING ROADS

The first surfaced roads in Britain were built by the Roman army. They were usually paved with stone and very straight, so that the army could march as fast as possible from one town to another, at the rate of about 30 kilometres a day. Roads were laid out using a tool called a **groma**. One soldier stood at a distance holding up a stick. Another soldier lined it up with two weighted strings on the groma. With the groma in the right position the soldiers could mark out a straight line for the road.

A Roman legionary wore a long shirt called a tunic, with armour over his chest and shoulders, and a helmet to protect his head. The armour had to be polished every time it got wet, to stop it rusting. On his feet he had sandals with nails on the soles to help grip the ground. In cold weather he might have worn woollen trousers, a cloak and leather boots. He carried two spears and a heavy, curved shield made of wood and leather. In his belt he had a short sword.

Soldiers trained very hard, with exercises twice a day. They served in the army for 25 years. They were not allowed to get married, but some did have girlfriends and children, who had to live outside the camp. When soldiers retired they could marry and were given money or a piece of land to farm.

Towns

The Romans brought the idea of towns to Britain. Many Romans liked to live in towns because it was easier to buy and sell things, and there was more to do. For the Britons it was very different to the country life they had known before the Romans came.

Roman towns in Britain were copies of towns in Italy, but were usually smaller. Five of the most important towns were Londinium (London), Camulodunum (Colchester), Eboracum (York), Glenuum (Gloucester) and Lindum (Lincoln).

Planned towns

Streets were straight and crossed each other at right angles in a grid pattern. At the centre was a big market square called a **forum**, where people went to meet each other and buy and sell food and crafts at open market stalls. There might also be entertainers such as jugglers and fortune tellers. Here in the forum rich people put up statues of emperors – the rulers of the Roman empire – and gods.

Around the forum was a temple, where people went to worship the gods, and a basilica, which was like a combined law court and town hall. These important buildings were made of stone, in Roman designs with tall columns.

◄ This painting shows how the Roman town of Silchester, in Hampshire, might have looked. At its centre was the forum. The buildings had red tiled roofs similar to those in many parts of southern Europe today.

These soldiers' toilets on Hadrian's Wall have separate channels for toilet waste and water for cleaning the body. The stone basins were for washing hands afterwards.

Romans knew that it was important to have clean water and a way to get rid of dirty water and toilet waste. Otherwise diseases could spread very quickly. Towns had public toilets, where people sat together. Drains carried the **sewage** away. Clean water came into the town through lead pipes and stone channels. People collected fresh water from a water pipe in the street.

Life in towns

Rich people lived in large houses that looked inwards to a garden, but most of the population lived in small houses or flats, with shops underneath. Town dwellers had time to go to the public baths, and watch entertainments in theatres and in stadiums called amphitheatres.

Life in towns was not always safe, and most towns had walls to defend those inside from enemies. The only way in was through gates which were closed at night.

▶ Wroxeter, known to the Romans as Viroconium, was a large town with a great forum and a bath house. After the Romans left Britain it was abandoned for ever, and walls like these are all that is left.

Jobs

The Roman period was the first time that many British craftworkers could live just by selling what they made. They didn't have to spend time growing their own food as well because they could settle in the town, working on one particular craft, and buy their food and other supplies in the market with the money they earned from their craftwork.

In Roman Britain there were many new jobs, such as making tiles or central heating systems for Roman-style houses. Britons who could read and write Latin worked in the towns. Some collected taxes for the Roman rulers.

Country life

In the countryside men, women and children worked on farms as they had done before the Romans arrived. Farmers kept pigs, goats, sheep and cattle, and grew wheat, barley, oats and beans. Some worked in their own houses, making wooden or iron farming tools or leather equipment for horses. Others ground flour to make bread.

◀ This carving on a Roman tombstone was found in Yorkshire and is now in the Yorkshire Museum in York. It shows a smith with hammer, tongs and anvil. There were many jobs for him to do, including making horseshoes, tools and weapons.

Women often spent their time at home looking after children, cooking, spinning wool and weaving cloth. Some worked in markets or shops, or as bath attendants. Rich women did not go out to work. They had slaves to look after the children and to do the housework and cooking.

Slaves and masters

Slaves were owned by their masters. In Roman times people became slaves after being captured in battle, or as a punishment for a crime, or by having slave parents. They were given their food and housing, but were not usually paid any money. Masters could sell them and their children.

Slaves did many hard jobs like mining or building, as well as all the work in the houses of the wealthy. Not all masters were cruel, and some slaves were treated almost like part of the family. A master could free a slave. Sometimes he might marry a female slave and give her her freedom.

▼ This bronze figure – found in County Durham and now in the British Museum – shows a farmer with a pair of oxen (large cattle). Oxen were used in Roman times for pulling carts, and for ploughing the soil so that crops could be planted.

▲ This Roman bronze lamp was found in the Roman town of Aldborough and is now in the museum there. It shows a slave boy asleep. He looks well-fed, as if he is well-treated by his master.

Buying and Selling

One reason the Romans came to Britain was for trade. The goods the Romans sold to the Britons came from other parts of the Roman empire, especially southern Europe, and included wine, oil, fish sauce, drinking glasses and fine decorated red pottery called Samian ware. In return the Britons sold wheat, iron, wool, hunting dogs, gold and slaves to the Romans.

All these goods had to be shipped across the sea to and from mainland Europe. Roman ships had square sails, and oars for steering. They could sail up to 160 kilometres a day, depending on the wind. Many of these trading ships docked in London, the busiest port in Roman Britain.

▼ In this Roman carving, men are unloading large pottery jars called amphorae from a ship. The amphorae may have contained wine or oil, which would then be taken to market.

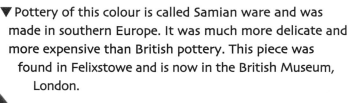
▼ Pottery of this colour is called Samian ware and was made in southern Europe. It was much more delicate and more expensive than British pottery. This piece was found in Felixstowe and is now in the British Museum, London.

Bartering and buying

Before the Romans came, money was not used much in Britain. The Britons grew their own food and made useful or decorative objects, which they bartered (swapped) with each other. Once they started living in the new Roman towns, they had little space to grow food. Many people began to work for money, which they spent in the markets and shops. More and more families were able to buy a few Roman objects – such as lamps, bowls and plates – for their houses.

There were no banks as we know them today, so people had to find a safe place at home to hide their money. Sometimes they buried it in a pot in the ground. If they died or left their homes in a hurry, their hoards of coins remained buried.

ROMAN COINS

Coins were made of metal – bronze, copper, silver or gold. The largest gold coin was called an aureus. The main silver coin was the denarius. There were 25 of these to one aureus. Bronze and copper coins were worth less. Coins had the head of the Roman emperor on one side, and often a symbol such as the spirit of peace or victory on the other. The Roman emperors put these symbols on the coins to show how powerful they were.

▲ We can still read the lettering on this Roman coin and see that the man's name is Claudius Caesar ('Emperor Claudius'). He was the emperor at the time of the invasion of Britain in AD 43.

Children and Family Life

Most children did not go to school but helped their parents in the house or at work. The whole family would get up at dawn, and have breakfast. The father might begin the day by going to a barber for a shave, before going on to work.

There were schools in the towns, but usually only boys went to them. Poor children often did not learn to read or write as their parents could not afford the school fees. Some rich families had a special slave called a pedagogue to teach and look after their sons.

▲ There was no paper in Roman times. Many students wrote with a special pointed tool called a stylus, as shown here, on a piece of soft, flat wax which was smoothed over afterwards. Other children practised writing on pieces of broken pottery.

Getting married

Girls could marry at the age of 12, and boys at 14. When a girl married, her parents had to pay the groom's family a sum of money called a dowry. The man could get a divorce if his wife had no children after they married, but he would have to return the dowry to her family.

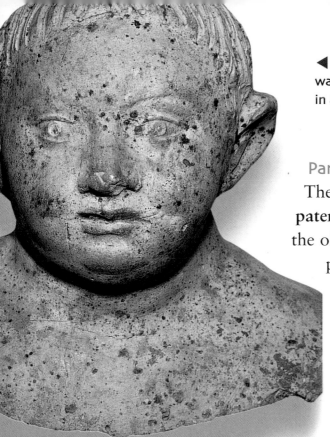

◀ Romans often made realistic statues of children. This boy was one of many who died young. He was buried in Colchester in around AD 60, and the statue was put up to mark his grave.

Parents and children

The oldest man in the family was known as the **pater familias** (father of the family). Because he was the oldest he was treated as the most important person in the house and could punish children by beating them.

Women usually looked after the home and children. If a woman had slaves she could get them to do most of the housework. A rich mother would probably have a lot of spare time for seeing friends.

▶ Lamps like this one found in Colchester (and now in the British Museum) were filled with oil. A wick was threaded through the hole and lit like a candle. Many lamps had decorations stamped on them. This one shows a Roman warship.

 AT NIGHT

Although rooms were sometimes lit by tiny oil lamps, homes would have been very dark at night. People went to bed soon after nightfall. Poor families lived and slept in one big, smoky room with an earth floor and hardly any windows. Richer families had bedrooms, and windows with glass in them.

Villas

Some Britons built new houses in the countryside, for which they copied Roman styles. These houses are called villas. Their owners were probably chiefs, or had become rich through trading with townspeople or the army.

Before the Romans came to Britain, everyone lived in round houses with mud walls and thatched roofs held up by wooden poles. Most people carried on living in these very simple buildings. But the Roman villas the rich built were much more like our houses today. They were rectangular, with tiles on the roof, glass in the windows and locks on the doors.

▲ A model of Fishbourne Roman Palace shows how it might have looked in the second century AD. Fishbourne, in West Sussex, is the largest Roman villa site ever found in Britain. Houses like these with their red roofs, rectangular shape, upstairs floors and gardens, were completely different from the buildings that existed before the Romans arrived.

Villa life

Life in a Roman villa must have been very comfortable. Many villas had heated floors and walls, warmed by an underfloor heating system called a **hypocaust** (see opposite). The villas also often had bath houses with hot and cold pools, where all the family could enjoy a bath together.

Villas usually had farms around them. Farm workers, villa slaves and servants (people who worked for wages) lived in much less comfort in wooden buildings and round houses nearby, and looked after the fields and animals. Only the owners lived like Romans in their villas.

Discovering villas today

Archaeologists think there are many Roman villas still waiting to be rediscovered. In parts of southern England there may be a villa every few kilometres. The villas we know about are mostly in places chosen for their beautiful views. Usually the stone from the walls was taken away centuries ago for use in other buildings, such as churches, but the foundations (bottoms of the walls) are still there under the soil.

▼ Inside Fishbourne Roman Palace a floor has crumbled away and you can see the heating system that was underneath. The stacks of tiles supported the floors, allowing hot air to move underneath and rise up through hollows in the walls.

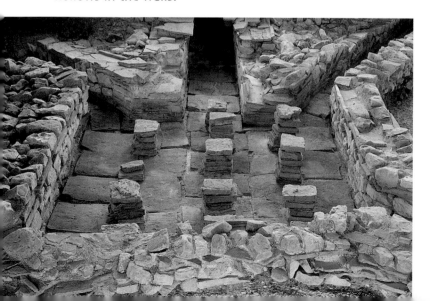

MOSAICS

The best rooms in villas and big town houses often had mosaic floors. Mosaics were made from tiny cubes of coloured stone called tesserae, arranged into patterns and pictures. Villa owners could choose their favourite pictures or scenes from popular stories. The mosaic artist would come to the villa and set the tesserae in a bed of sand and cement. Some artists were experts who travelled all over Europe; others made mistakes which you can still see.

▲ A mosaic floor in the dining room of Lullingstone Villa, Kent. At the top and bottom are scenes of people and animals from famous Roman stories. In between are patterns which the Romans believed brought good luck.

Food and Drink

Many of the foods that were eaten regularly in Roman Britain, such as bread, grapes and honey, are familiar to us today. Rich Britons could also buy food and drink from all over the Roman empire, including wine, figs and olive oil from warmer countries.

The Romans introduced some new foods to Britain, such as sweet chestnuts and chicken, but they did not have many things we now take for granted – like tomatoes and potatoes. Instead of sugar, they used honey to make food sweeter. Roman Britons also ate a lot of oysters and shellfish, and even snails.

Romans liked their food to be strongly flavoured. A spicy sauce, made from fish guts, was added to make food more tasty. Some Roman foods seem strange to us today. How would you like to try dormice, or a mixture of anchovies and honey?

▲ Roman saucepans were sometimes made of bronze. This one is beautifully decorated and must have belonged to a rich family. It was found in the Isle of Ely, Cambridgeshire, and is now in the British Museum.

Cooking and storing food

Only large houses had proper kitchens, with stoves heated by a wood fire. Everyone else cooked over a simple fire more like a barbecue, or ate food from market stalls and bars. Because there were no fridges, the only way of keeping food cool was to place it in water or in a dark place away from the heat of the sun. Meat and fish were stored in salt to make them last longer.

This is how a Roman kitchen might have looked, with jugs of oil and wine, and a pan on an iron grid heated by charcoal. Earthenware pots often broke when they were heated, but bronze pans were better. These pots are in the Colchester Castle Museum.

Roman meals

Roman Britons did not use knives or forks to help them eat their food. Sometimes they used spoons but usually they picked up food with their fingers. Most people ate three meals a day, with bread and fruit for breakfast, and cold meat, vegetables and bread for lunch.

A ROMAN FEAST

Rich people sometimes held special big feasts, or banquets. They lay on couches as they ate. The food was placed on a low table in front of them. The first course would often have salad, eggs or shellfish. Then came the main course, including dishes of fish, meat and chicken. When the diners had finished, slaves would remove the whole table and bring in the third course – fruit, nuts and honey cakes – on a clean table.

The main meal of the day was eaten at around 4 o'clock in the afternoon and was called cena. This often included fish, meat and vegetables.

In this model of a Roman dining room, a wealthy woman is lying on a couch and enjoying some fruit at the end of a meal. Her slaves will clear away the dishes when she has finished.

Clothes and Fashion

Roman clothing was quite comfortable, loose and light, but not very warm. People used brooches to hold their clothes together. There were no zips or buttons, and it was difficult to do any complicated sewing with the clumsy bone needles the Romans used. Clothes were usually made of wool, linen, leather or fur, or sometimes cotton or silk from abroad.

Unlike the Britons, most Romans never wore trousers. Only soldiers and farm-workers wore them – when it was really cold. Instead, Romans had **tunics,** tightened around the middle with a belt. On special occasions important male Roman citizens might wear togas. These were long pieces of cloth draped around the body rather like a sari. Women wore longer dresses over their tunics.

▶ Members of the Ermine Street Guard re-enactment society dressed in Roman costume. Brooches were worn near the shoulders to pin together long, loose pieces of cloth.

► Both men and women wore rings. A bride wore a ring on the third finger of her left hand, as people do today. This gold Roman ring was found at Backworth in Northumberland and is now in the British Museum.

Many people probably went around barefoot. The most popular type of shoe was a leather sandal. This was tied up with long laces, and probably took quite a long time to put on.

Jewellery and make-up

Many people, rich and poor, wore lucky animal charms, earrings, beads and rings. A rich woman had a lot of spare time to make herself look beautiful. For make-up she used red wine for her cheeks and lips, and powdered chalk to make her skin look pale. The Romans thought that being suntanned made them look like poor farm-workers.

▼ Women often styled their hair with a curled fringe, in a bun or parted in the middle. These figures are called mother goddesses and probably look like Roman mothers did. This stone carving was found in Cirencester and is now in the Corinium Museum there.

 ## HAIRSTYLES

People in Britain learned about the latest hair styles by seeing faces on coins. In the early days of Roman rule men had short hair, and shaved their faces. Later the Emperor Hadrian made it fashionable to have longer hair and a beard. Women and girls had long hair in complicated styles, and often wore hairpins and decorations. Some women dyed their hair or curled it with heated tongs, while others wore wigs made from real hair.

Gods and Customs

The Romans allowed most people in the empire to follow their own religion. Roman Britain had many religions. People often worshipped water spirits and animals such as boars, like their British ancestors had done, as well as new gods the Romans brought with them.

There were many Roman gods and goddesses. The Romans believed that each of them looked after different things or people. Minerva was the goddess of wisdom, war and crafts. Jupiter was god of the sky, while his wife Juno protected women.

Sacrifices and shrines

In towns everyone was supposed to go to the main temple to worship the emperor – who was a god to the Romans – and the other main Roman gods and goddesses like Jupiter, Juno and Minerva. Sometimes they had special processions to the temples where they would make **sacrifices** by killing animals such as chickens or goats as a way of giving them to the gods.

▲ On this stone tablet found at Bisley in Gloucestershire, Mars – the Roman god of war – holds a spear and shield. The month of March is named after him. This tablet is now in Gloucester City Museum.

In Roman houses, people often kept small statues of Lar, the god of the home, in a special place called a shrine. Every day the women would put flowers and food in the shrine, as a gift to Lar.

Burying the dead

When people died their bodies were either buried, or cremated (burnt) and their ashes buried. Food and drink were placed in graves to help the dead on their journey to the **underworld**. A coin was placed in their mouths to pay for the boat to take them across the River Styx, the river the Romans believed that the dead had to cross to reach the underworld.

CHRISTIANITY SPREADS

In the early centuries AD Christianity spread through the Roman empire. Because Christians believed in only one God and refused to worship the Roman emperor, the Romans put many of them in prison and even killed them. But by the 4th century, Christianity had become the religion of the Roman empire and even the emperor became a Christian.

▲ This 4th-century painting in Lullingstone Villa, Kent, is the only Christian wall painting dating from Roman times that has been found in Britain. The figures have crosses on their robes.

▼ Carrawburgh Temple near Hadrian's Wall. Worshippers from the soldiers' camp nearby placed food for the god Mithras on the three altars. Archaeologists have found remains of chicken bones, candle-holders and scented pine cones there.

Clean and Healthy Living

Although the Romans didn't know about diseases, they understood that washing and clean water were important for good health. In many places they built drains to carry the sewage away from the towns.

The Romans loved bathing in public bath houses. In the towns, people who could afford it went there every day to meet their friends. This was like going to a gym, a swimming pool and a sauna all in one. Slaves kept the fires going to heat the baths.

When people went to the bath house, they began by getting undressed and doing some exercises. They would then relax in the warm room (called the tepidarium) and the hot room (caldarium). Then a slave would clean and massage them. The slave scraped off all the sweat and dirt with a shaped piece of metal called a strigil. Finally the bathers would freshen up with a dip in a cold pool, or frigidarium. While relaxing in the bath house, they might play a game of dice with a friend.

◀ Warm springs supply the water for the Great Bath in Bath, once one of the largest Roman baths in Europe. In more modern times it was rebuilt in Roman style, surrounded by columns and statues.

GETTING WELL

Most doctors in Roman times were Greek. They used medicines made of plants, animals and minerals. People also believed the gods had powers to cure them, and so carried out special ceremonies or made spells. Afterwards they offered the gods a model of the part of their body that had been healed, such as a leg or a finger. Soldiers were well looked after by army doctors and had healthy food. If they did not get wounded in battle, they often lived to a good age.

▼ In this Roman carving the man sitting on the left is an apothecary, who is selling herbs and treatments for illnesses. Some ingredients were ground up and made into pills.

Disease and death

Even though the Romans were clean there were still many diseases that spread rapidly around the towns. Women often died having babies, while many babies and small children died in infancy. About one person in two died before the age of 40, but some lucky people lived to be 70 or 80.

◄ A set of Roman surgical tools, found in Colchester by the Colchester Archaeological Trust. Doctors used several types of instruments for operations, including forceps and tweezers for pulling, and scalpels for cutting. Operations would have been very painful as patients were awake as the doctor worked.

Entertainments

Most Roman towns had a huge oval stadium called an amphitheatre, which seated thousands. This was used for all kinds of entertainment including military displays and races.

Many people enjoyed cruel entertainments like watching criminals being put to death, and contests between specially trained slave fighters called gladiators. There were different types of gladiators. A retiarius fought with a net and trident (a three-pointed spear). His opponent might be a secutor, who wore a helmet and used a sword. The two gladiators would fight until one of them was defeated. Usually the loser was killed in the fight. If he survived, the spectators decided his fate. If they pointed their thumbs up he was allowed to live, but if they gave the thumbs down he was killed. A gladiator who won five fights in a row was freed from slavery as a reward.

Entertainment in the theatre

Some towns, such as St Albans, Canterbury and Colchester, also had a theatre. People sat on steps to watch plays or listen to singing.

▼ In this mosaic found in Bignor Villa in West Sussex, two gladiators are fighting. On the left a secutor defends himself against a retiarius, who has a trident and net, while on the right stands the umpire (or rudarius).

There were serious plays called tragedies, as well as comedies and **mime** shows. The costumes and masks helped the audience understand the story. For example, purple clothes meant the actor was playing the part of a young man, and an actor wore a red wig to show he was acting the part of a slave.

Hunting

In the countryside, hunting for wild boar and deer was a popular sport. The Romans introduced fallow deer from abroad so that people could hunt them.

GAMES AND TOYS

Many children had games and toys. These included board games with counters and dice, dolls made of clay, wood or cloth, wooden hoops, balls, spinning tops and toy animals made of pottery or metal. Some children learned to play a musical instrument, such as a lyre (like a small harp) or a set of pipes. Adults liked to bet, sometimes by rolling dice and guessing which number would come up.

▲ This game has a stone board marked with squares, and red and white counters. The red counters are made from pieces of Samian pottery. The dice are just the same as those we use today. The game was found at Corbridge, a military base on Hadrian's Wall. It is now in the Corbridge Roman Site Museum.

◄ You can still see the shape of this Roman theatre at St Albans. The banks were originally covered with wooden seats, with enough space for 2,000 people to watch plays and other entertainments.

The End of Roman Britain

Nearly 400 years after the invasion of Britain, the Roman empire began to collapse. The army had to go to fight on the other side of Europe. Saxon warriors from what is now Germany began to sail ships across the North Sea to attack British towns and villas.

Without the Roman army to buy their products, British farmers and shopkeepers became poorer and there were fewer jobs making luxuries such as jewellery.

Many people had to go back to growing their own food. They left the towns, and soon the buildings started to fall down. The roads fell into disrepair, too. Nothing as good was built again for 1,300 years.

◄ After the Roman army left, many people took away the stones from Roman buildings to make houses, but some ruins still stand today. This is a round tower of a fort – Burgh Castle in Norfolk. Burgh Castle was one of ten forts the Romans built on the east and south coasts to keep invaders from Germany and Denmark out of Britain.

WHAT THE ROMANS LEFT

There are signs of the Romans all around us. Some clocks use Roman numbers like X (10), V (5) and I (1). Some very straight main roads follow the line of Roman roads. Many big buildings like town halls and museums are built in a Roman style, with columns and arches.

The names of places can tell us that the Romans built them. The words 'chester', 'cester' and 'caster' in a town's name – like Chichester, Leicester or Lancaster – mean that it was once a Roman fort.

Slowly, life in Britain became more like it was before the Romans arrived. The Saxons moved into farms in the south and east of England, bringing a new language with them. The English we speak today contains both Latin and Saxon words.

▲ In a few places in Britain you can see the original surface of Roman roads. This road crosses Blackstone Edge near Manchester.

Roman remains

Most Roman buildings have disappeared, but underground there are many Roman remains. Some walls and floors have been dug up, along with bones, pottery and objects made from stone, but soft materials like wood, leather and cloth have usually rotted away.

▼ These archaeologists are uncovering the walls and rooms of a villa at Barcombe in East Sussex. The villa was discovered when people noticed the ploughed field was full of pieces of Roman bricks and tiles.

Timeline

753 BC Rome is founded, according to legend.

AD 43 Roman Emperor Claudius invades Britain.

49 Colchester becomes the first capital of Roman Britain.

60 A chief of the Britons called Boudicca burns down Colchester, London and St Albans, killing thousands of people. She later dies after a battle with the Romans.

122-127 Hadrian's Wall is built across northern England.

139-142 The Antonine Wall is begun across part of Scotland.

around 200 A wall and gates are built to protect London, the new capital.

212 All free people in Britain are made Roman citizens.

313 Emperor Constantine accepts Christianity across the Roman Empire.

from 300 Roman Britain attacked by people from north of Hadrian's Wall and in the east by Saxons and Jutes from northern Europe.

410 Roman army leaves Britain.

Places to Visit

Bignor Roman Villa, near Pulborough, West Sussex
Beautiful mosaics, and the bases of the villa's walls.

Caerleon Roman Fortress, near Newport, Wales
The site of a Roman fortress town, with barracks where soldiers lived, baths and one of the best examples of an amphitheatre in Britain.

Chedworth Roman Villa, near Cirencester, Gloucestershire
A large villa, with mosaics, a hypocaust and a water shrine.

Colchester Castle Museum, Colchester, Essex
Many Roman objects that have been found in the Roman town. You can try on Roman togas and helmets.

Corinium Museum, Cirencester, Gloucestershire
A museum showing what Roman rooms looked like, and many things the Romans used in everyday life.

Fishbourne Roman Palace, near Chichester, West Sussex
The biggest Roman villa ever found in northern Europe, with mosaics and a Roman garden.

Grosvenor Museum and Dewa Roman Experience, Chester, Cheshire
Find out about Roman Chester, and see a collection of Roman tombstones. Dewa Roman Experience is an exciting look at Roman times, with sights, sounds and smells of the streets, fortresses and bath houses.

Housesteads and Vindolanda forts, Hadrian's Wall, Northumberland
The best Roman forts in Britain, on the long stone wall built by Emperor Hadrian with a good museum at Vindolanda. There are several other Roman forts and museums nearby.

Lullingstone Roman Villa, near Eynsford, Kent
A villa with mosaics, wall paintings, a hypocaust and a very unusual Christian shrine.

Museum of London, London Wall, London
Wonderful free museum, with Roman shops, the inside of a Roman house, coins, jewellery, sculptures and many other objects.

Roman Baths, Bath, Somerset
A holy hot spring where the Romans worshipped Minerva, and took baths.

Verulamium Museum, St Albans, Hertfordshire
Tells the story of the Roman town of Verulamium. Nearby you can visit a Roman theatre, see a mosaic floor and find the Roman walls built around the town.

Wroxeter Roman City, near Shrewsbury, Shropshire
Once home to 6,000 people, it now just has the ruins of the bath house.

Glossary

anvil a block on which a smith hammers metal.

amphitheatre an oval-shaped stadium for entertainments.

archaeologist someone who digs up and studies ancient remains.

Britons the people who lived in Britain before the Romans came.

empire a group of countries ruled by an emperor or empress.

forum the big market square at the centre of a Roman town.

groma an instrument used to lay out straight lines for building roads.

hypocaust a central heating system, with hot air moving along channels under the floor.

mime a theatrical performance using gestures instead of words.

pater familias the oldest man, who was the head of the family.

re-enactment society a group of people who get together to recreate life in the past.

sacrifice the act of killing or giving something as a gift, often to the gods.

sewage dirty water and toilet waste.

shrine a small area, often in a house, where people honoured the gods.

slave someone, often a prisoner or a son or daughter of another slave, who belonged to a master and usually had to do hard work without getting paid.

tunic a garment worn like a shirt, but covering the tops of the legs too.

underworld the place under the ground where the Romans believed people went after they died.

villa a large house in the country, often in farmland.

Books and Websites

Books

Moira Butterfield, *Going to War in Roman Times*, Franklin Watts, 2000

Peter Chrisp, *In Roman Britain*, Hodder Wayland, 2001

Peter Chrisp, *Look Inside a Roman Villa*, Hodder Wayland, 2002

Alison Cooper, *Roman Britain*, Hodder Wayland, 2001

Mike Corbishley and Mick Cooper, *Real Romans - Digital Time Traveller* book/CD-ROM, English Heritage/TAG Learning, 1999

Richard Wood, *On the Trail of the Romans in Britain*, Franklin Watts, 1999

Rachel Wright, *Craft Topics: The Romans*, Franklin Watts, 2001

Map of Roman Britain, Ordnance Survey, 2000

Websites

www.bbc.co.uk/schools/romans
BBC website on the Romans and their history, written for Key Stage 2. Links to the Romans in Scotland and other BBC websites.

www.britarch.ac.uk/yac
The young archaeologists' club (for 9-16s), with details of local clubs, events, competitions and more. Organised by the Council of British Archaeology.

www.english-heritage.org.uk
Information on sites owned by English Heritage. Among these are many Roman buildings you can visit. Follow the Kids link.

www.esg.ndirect.co.uk
All about the Ermine Street Guard, who dress up as Roman soldiers and perform military exercises. They take part in many events across Britain.

www.pyrrha.demon.co.uk
Lots of Roman topics and ideas.

www.romansinsussex.co.uk
Roman life in Sussex, explained by the Sussex Archaeological Society. Level 1 in the site is designed specially for ages 7–11.

Index